CONTENTS

CHAPTER 1

What is Monarchy?

Queen Victoria, King Richard the Lionheart, King Arthur, King Louis XIV of France, Empress Catherine of Russia – history has made kings, queens, emperors and empresses famous. The individuals who are given these titles can be described as monarchs, a useful general word that covers them all. Monarchs have also been known by many other titles. Over the centuries, pharaohs, caesars, kaisers, tsars, shahs, khans and sultans have reigned and made their mark on history.

'Monarchy' is an equally useful general word. It describes any form of government in which a monarch holds the highest office. In a monarchy, a titled individual such as a king is the sovereign (supreme ruler) and head of state, and has normally inherited his, or her, position. This is what makes a monarchy different from the main alternative system of government in modern times – a republic.

In a republic, a president generally holds the highest office. In some countries the president may have seized power by force, but in most instances he or she will have been elected. The present monarch of the United Kingdom (UK) is Queen Elizabeth II, who became queen in

A portrait of royal authority:
Queen Elizabeth I of England
(1558–1603), holding the orb
(right) and sceptre.

Greek origins
'Monarchy' comes from the Greek word 'monarchia', meaning 'rule of one'. The ancient Greeks were the first people to classify and analyse political systems.

SYSTEMS OF GOVERNMENT

MONARCHY

Nathaniel Harris

Evans

First published in paperback in 2009 by Evans Brothers Limited
2A Portman Mansions
Chiltern Street
London W1U 6NR

Planned and produced for Evans Brothers by Book Factory Limited.

British Library Cataloguing in Publication Data
Harris, Nathaniel
Monarchy, - (Systems of government)
1. Monarchy - Juvenile literature
2. Monarchy - History - Juvenile literature
I. Title
321'6

Printed in Hong Kong

ISBN 9780237539320

Editor: Patience Coster
Designer: Jane Hawkins
Illustrations: Stefan Chabluk
Consultant: Michael Rawcliffe

We are grateful to the following for permission to reproduce photographs: Archivo Iconografico. S.A./Corbis 21, 23; The Bridgeman Art Library 6, 11, 14, 19; The Bridgeman Art Library/Archives Charmet 10; The Bridgeman Art Library/Ashmolean Museum, University of Oxford 15; The Bridgeman Art Library/City of Edinburgh Museums and Art Galleries, Scotland 9; The Bridgeman Art Library/Egyptian National Museum, Cairo 13; The Bridgeman Art Library/Leeds Museum and Art Galleries 22; Corbis *front cover* and 5; Gideon Mendel/Corbis 33; Giraudon/The Bridgeman Art Library 12; Hulton-Deutsch Collection/Corbis 38; Mian Khursheed/Reuters/Corbis 31; Reuters/Corbis 28; Susana Vera/Reuters/Corbis 30; Tim Graham/Corbis 29, *title page* and 36, 43; Topham/ImageWorks 20; Topham Picturepoint 4, *front cover* and 24, 25, 34, 39, 42; Topham/Polfoto 40; Topham/The British Library/HIP 8; Topham/UPPA 27, 41; Vittoriano Rastelli/Corbis 17.

In this book dates often appear in brackets after the names of individual monarchs. These are the monarch's reign dates, not birth and death dates. Dates are also written using BCE and CE, instead of BC and AD which are based on the Christian calendar. BCE means 'Before the Common Era' and it replaces BC ('Before Christ'). CE means 'in the Common Era' and it replaces AD ('Anno Domini' – 'in the year of our Lord').

1952 following the death of her father, King George VI. By contrast, George W. Bush became president of the USA in 2001 after winning a nationwide election. Bush, like all US presidents, held power for only four years but was allowed to stand for re-election. He won again, and was consequently served for a further four years. He was succeeded by Barack Obama in 2009.

Royal inheritance

In most monarchies, the monarch reigns until he or she dies. (However, some monarchs have chosen, or have been forced, to abdicate – to resign the crown and allow a successor to take their place.) The crown is generally hereditary (inherited as if it were property) and passes from one member of the ruling family to the next. The order of inheritance follows rules that reflect the origins of monarchy in a male-dominated world. Almost everywhere, the oldest son of the monarch inherits the throne, even if he has an older sister. If there are no sons, the oldest daughter inherits, which is why Queen Elizabeth (the older of King George VI's two daughters) is the present sovereign of the UK.

If the monarch has no children, the nearest relation succeeds, with the same male-first principle continuing to be followed.

Traditional royal pomp: the gilded state coach is used by British monarchs on important occasions such as the opening of parliament. In this instance, Queen Elizabeth II and her husband Prince Philip are travelling to St Paul's Cathedral, London, for a service to mark the Queen's Golden Jubilee (fiftieth anniversary) in June 2002.

King-making

Almost all monarchs go through some kind of ceremony at the beginning of their reigns. The most common ceremony is a coronation (literally 'crowning'), which either creates or recognises the monarch's royal authority. A Roman emperor was dressed in a purple cloak, and a laurel wreath was placed on his head. Then the acclamation followed – shouts that signified acceptance of the new monarch.

The Roman Emperor Constantine (307–337 CE) made the crown the chief symbol of his office. Then, in seventh-century Spain, the king was anointed with holy oil, following the practice recorded in the Bible. Other insignia (symbols of authority) were introduced, notably the mitre, sceptre and orb. Coronations became, and have remained, lavish, spectacular, and for many people deeply emotional, events.

However, the rules of inheritance have varied slightly from place to place. For example, when France was a monarchy (c.500–1848), the Salic Law excluded females from succeeding in any circumstances. Not surprisingly, most monarchs in history have been male. In spite of this, some of the most celebrated rulers have been women, from Hatshepsut in ancient Egypt (1479–1458 BCE) to Queen Elizabeth I of England (1558–1603) and the Empress Catherine of Russia (1762–1796).

Until very recent times, almost all states were monarchies. The exceptions were mainly very small states, where it was possible for many citizens to take some part in government. In most places, slow communications and scattered populations meant that the permanent authority of a single individual was a more effective way of getting things done. Monarchy also had the advantage of continuity. When a monarch died, the next in line took over immediately, without any break in authority. This was symbolised by the ceremonial announcement, made when a French monarch died: 'The king is dead: long live the king!'

Royalty and nobility

Most societies based on monarchy have been divided into ranks or classes with widely different powers and privileges. This arrangement is often shown as a pyramid-

This painting from around 1620 shows how royal authority is handed down from one generation to the next. Akbar, the sixteenth-century Mughal emperor of India, passes the crown from his son Jahangir to his grandson Shah Jahan.

shaped diagram with the monarch at its top and the majority of people, or commoners, at its base. In between come a number of privileged groups, of which the nobility, or aristocracy, are ranked directly below the monarch. Apart from the monarch's children (princes and princesses), nobles have titles such as duke, earl, baron and lord, or their equivalents in other languages. At times, nobles have conspired or rebelled against monarchs. But the highest noble families are usually closely related to the royal family, and the monarch is the giver of titles and other honours. So when the idea of monarchy is attacked, the nobility has generally rushed to its defence.

When they have been established for a long time, royal and noble families come to be thought of as special people. In Britain, they used to be described as 'blue blooded', which implied that they were different from, and somehow better than, ordinary red-blooded people. The authority of a monarchy is greatly strengthened when the monarch is generally believed to be a special, superior being.

Divine rulers

In many cases, this idea has been very powerful because the monarch has been seen as a religious or divinely approved figure. Some monarchs have been gods or god-like. This was true, for

Lords of the Earth

For centuries, nomadic tribes moved over vast areas of northern Asia, grazing their flocks. Their superb horsemanship and sharp-shooting with bow and arrow made them fearsome warriors. Whenever a gifted leader managed to unite the tribes, they posed a serious threat to the settled civilisations of Asia. The most successful of all nomad leaders was Temujin, creator of the Mongol Empire. He is better known by the title of Genghis Khan ('Lord of the Earth'). Temujin was given this title in 1206, when he united the Mongol tribes and set out on an extraordinary career of conquest. By the time of his death in 1227, Temujin's empire stretched from northern China to Persia and Eastern Europe. His sons were equally successful, and his grandson, Kublai Khan (1259–94), became emperor of China. The Mongol Empire broke up soon afterwards, but later Mongol conquerors included Timur (1370–1405) and Babur (1526–30).

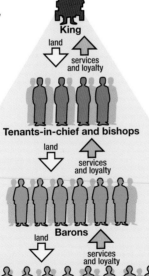

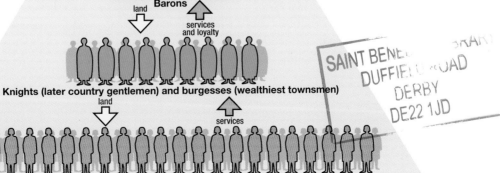

Pyramid of power: how authority and benefits flowed between the different levels of medieval society.

King

land / services and loyalty

Tenants-in-chief and bishops

land / services and loyalty

Barons

land / services and loyalty

Knights (later country gentlemen) and burgesses (wealthiest townsmen)

land / services

Peasants and town workers

This fifteenth-century painting shows the coronation of a medieval king. The crown is placed on the king's head in the presence of four bishops. Most of those present are also members of the clergy. The religious aspect of coronations made kings sacred figures in the eyes of many subjects.

example, of the pharaohs who ruled ancient Egypt. The emperors of Japan were also worshipped as divine until 1945; then, after Japan's defeat in the Second World War, the victors (the USA and its allies) made Emperor Hirohito admit to the Japanese people that he was not a god.

Most monarchs have not claimed to be divine, but have relied heavily on the support of the state religion. This was displayed in rituals and ceremonies, carried out with great pomp. In Europe, a new monarch's right to rule was proclaimed by a coronation, held in a cathedral or abbey and conducted by the Church in the presence of the highest nobility.

Tradition, inheritance and religious ceremonial worked together to make it appear to the people that monarchs had a right to rule. Many individuals developed an intense loyalty to their sovereigns, and were prepared to fight and die in their defence. In 1642, the unpopular policies of King Charles I of England led to a civil war between supporters of the king and of parliament (an assembly with an important role in making

❝Not all the water in the rough rude sea Can wash the balm from an anointed king; The breath of worldly men cannot depose The deputy elected by the Lord❞

These lines come from Richard II, a play written by William Shakespeare in about 1595. Fearing that he may be deposed by his subjects, the king comforts himself with the belief that he has a divine right to rule because he is God's deputy on earth.

laws). When the war started, many who had disagreed with the king's actions rallied to his side, feeling that they could not fight against 'His Sacred Majesty'. Later, Charles's exiled descendants found devoted supporters, known as Jacobites (*see panel*), over several generations.

Wielding power

Until recent centuries, monarchy aroused feelings of awe almost everywhere in the world. But the actual power wielded by monarchs has varied greatly. In some states, the monarch was a figurehead, without any significant authority. In others, he or she was 'the first among equals' – really just the leading noble in a society run by and for the nobility. In eighteenth-century Poland, the elected king could do almost nothing without the consent of the nobility, even in an emergency. The country lacked decisive political leadership and, largely as a result, by 1795 had been divided between the powerful neighbouring states of Prussia, Russia and Austria.

'Divine' monarchs were not necessarily powerful either. In some instances, their sacred status meant they

Followers of Prince Charles Edward Stuart ('Bonnie Prince Charlie') raise their glasses in a toast to him. The Prince failed to regain the throne for his father, but the painting shows the romantic appeal of his story and of the Jacobites' loyalty to his family.

Jacobite loyalty

In seventeenth-century England and Scotland, crown and parliament were frequently in conflict. In 1688, King James II was driven into exile and his son was barred from succeeding. The exiled king and his descendants made a number of attempts to recover the throne, relying on the loyalty to 'the rightful king' still felt by many people. Their supporters, known as Jacobites (Jacobus is Latin for James), took part in several rebellions. In 1745, James's grandson, Prince Charles Edward ('Bonnie Prince Charlie'), led a Scottish Jacobite army deep into England before being forced back and defeated. The Jacobites failed, but their loyalty to their cause has always found admirers.

were cut off from any kind of practical activity. For centuries, the Japanese emperors were revered figures who lived quietly in their palaces while the country was actually ruled by a Shogun, the leader of the dominant clan.

Most monarchs in history have wielded more power than these Japanese emperors. At the opposite extreme were rulers whose authority was almost unlimited. Their absolute power enabled them to kill or reward whomever they pleased, and to sacrifice their subjects (the people they ruled) in great wars or huge construction schemes. Such monarchs are often described as autocrats, or despots.

Famous autocrats include Shi Huangdi (221–210 BCE), the first Chinese emperor, who built the Great Wall of China, and Tsar Peter I of Russia (1682–1725), who created the great city of St Petersburg. Both achievements cost thousands of lives. Some autocrats have been moderate, well-meaning rulers, but access to such unchecked power has generally encouraged more vicious qualities. Several Roman emperors killed so many enemies, or people they believed to be their enemies, that no one felt safe. Their reigns usually ended when the emperor was assassinated or overthrown by his subjects.

A great many monarchies fell between these extremes of helplessness and

The imperial line

A series of monarchs belonging to the same family is known as a dynasty. Some dynasties have ruled for centuries. The longest lasting of all European dynasties was that of the Habsburgs.

From 1438 to 1806 the Habsburgs held the title of Holy Roman Emperor, which made them the recognised overlords of Germany and certain other parts of central Europe. They constantly added to their territories by making shrewd marriage alliances with other royal and noble families, and they reached the height of their power during the sixteenth and early seventeenth centuries. In the nineteenth century the Habsburgs still ruled an Austrian empire covering much of south-east Europe. Catastrophic defeats during the First World War (1914–18) led to the break-up of the empire and the abdication of Charles I, the last Habsburg emperor.

despotism. The monarch had great power, but was supposed to act according to the law. When vital decisions had to be taken, he or she might be expected to consult some group of wise advisers, or nobles, or other representatives of the realm. In England, the king was advised from the thirteenth century onwards by an assembly of great lords, leading churchmen and representatives of the wealthier classes. By the seventeenth century this assembly, known as parliament, played such an important role in making laws and raising taxes that it came into conflict with the crown and eventually took over many royal powers.

Although the authority of monarchs and monarchies might vary, monarchy as an institution remained essentially unchallenged until about 1770. Then, new political ideas and social changes began to have a tremendous impact. Over the next two centuries, many monarchies disappeared. Most of those that survived became constitutional monarchies – more or less democratic states, with elected governments, where the monarch had a limited but definite role to play.

In the twenty-first century, there are relatively few monarchies left in the world. Those that remain, however, are surprisingly different from one another, reflecting their varied and colourful history.

A life-size terracotta figure from the tomb of the first Chinese emperor, who died in 210 BCE. The kneeling soldier originally held a real crossbow.

A DESPOTIC EMPEROR

Ancient China was divided into many rival kingdoms. In 221 BCE, Zheng, ruler of the Qin kingdom, subdued them all and proclaimed himself Shi Huangdi, or First Emperor. He ruthlessly imposed his will on China. Severe laws, heavy taxes and a network of roads and canals bound the kingdom together. A 4,000-kilometre-long Great Wall was built to protect the northern frontier, using forced labourers who died in tens of thousands. All books except histories of Qin were burned, and scholars who protested were buried alive. When Shi Huangdi died in 210 BCE, he was buried in an enormous tomb, guarded by a 'Terracotta Army' – thousands of life-size pottery figures of soldiers, horses and chariots. Later Chinese people detested Shi Huangdi as a tyrant, but also admired him for unifying their country.

Magic touch

The sacred character of kingship remained strong until recent times. In England, as late as the eighteenth century, being touched by the monarch was believed to cure a tubercular disease called scrofula. For that reason, the disease was also known as 'the king's evil'.

CHAPTER 2

Early Monarchies

Nobody knows exactly when the first monarchies were founded. But monarchy is generally believed to have appeared when early societies became complex, and specialised groups such as nobles, warriors, priests and farmers developed. Such societies needed greater organisation, and a single individual – a monarch – emerged to control and direct them.

The first civilisations

Monarchies already existed by the time the first civilisations appeared, in about 3000 BCE. Their centres were the lands of Sumer in Mesopotamia (present-day Iraq) and Egypt. Great rivers – the Tigris, the Euphrates and the Nile – flowed through these regions, and large-scale efforts were made to control them so that they fertilised the land and made it fruitful. The organisation this required went along with the development of governments, taxes, armies and written records, and with the growth of cities and the building of palaces and temples. Societies that possess most or all of such advanced features are known as civilisations.

In about 1500 BCE, a new civilisation developed independently in northern China, beginning a tradition that was to remain almost unbroken for 3,500 years. Gradually, ideas and skills from Mesopotamia, Egypt and China spread to other lands, including India, Asia Minor (modern Turkey), Crete, and eastern Mediterranean states such as Canaan, Israel, Judah and Phoenicia.

The bronze head of a ruler from Akkad, an early state in southern Mesopotamia. Some believe it is a portrait of Sargon I, a conqueror who ruled around 2300 BCE.

God-kings

In all of these early civilisations, the king was regarded as a special, sacred person, utterly different from the rest of the people. He was the all-powerful ruler of the land and also its supreme religious figure. It was believed that he alone could make direct contact with the gods, ensuring that they would favour his people. The king was himself godlike. In fact the kings of Egypt, known from about 1539 BCE as pharaohs, were believed to be literally divine, since each pharaoh was one of the greatest of the gods, Horus, in human form.

Sacred and all-powerful early kings gathered enormous wealth. Most of it has disappeared, but in the twentieth century archaeologists made some amazing discoveries. Beautifully crafted objects, rich in gold and other precious materials and dating from about 2600 BCE, were dug up among the remains of the Sumerian city of Ur in Iraq. The tomb of the pharaoh Tutankhamun contained even more spectacular finds. It was the only Egyptian royal tomb ever discovered with all its contents intact. Tutankhamun was around eighteen when he died (in about 1327 BCE) and had not been very important, yet his tomb was crammed with fabulous treasures.

One of many treasures found in the tomb of the boy pharaoh Tutankhamun, who died around 1327 BCE. This bejewelled gold pectoral (chest ornament) displays a royal vulture.

3000 BCE
Narmer becomes the first king of a united Egypt

1525–1479 BCE
Tuthmosis I and Tuthmosis II create an Egyptian empire in Nubia, to the south of Egypt, and in the Middle East

1473 BCE Hatshepsut proclaimed pharaoh

30 BCE
Death of Cleopatra, Egypt's last queen; Egypt becomes part of the Roman Empire

2500 BCE
Cheops builds the Great Pyramid, largest of all Egyptian pyramids

1550 BCE
Ahmose liberates Egypt from occupation by a people called the Hyksos and founds the 'New Kingdom'

1458–1425 BCE
Reign of Tuthmosis III, greatest of all Egyptian conquerors

1274 BCE
Ramesses II leads the Egyptians at the battle of Kadesh in Syria

3000 BCE **TIMELINE:**   2000 BCE   1000 BCE   BCE | CE
GREAT RULERS OF ANCIENT EGYPT

1352–1336 BCE
The pharaoh Akhenaten introduces the worship of a single god, the Aten

1336–1327 BCE
Under the boy pharaoh Tutankhamun the old religion of many gods is restored

13

A pharaoh's monuments to his own glory: the gigantic statue, and the remains of a mighty temple, are among many built by Ramesses II between 1279 and 1213 BCE.

Empire builders

The warrior-kings of Assyria, in northern Iraq, were among history's most ruthless conquerors. From the ninth century BCE, kings such as Tiglath-pileser III, Sargon II and Esarhaddon conquered a vast empire that for a time even included Egypt. The fighting qualities and cruelty of the Assyrians are seen in their great stone carvings, dedicated to sieges, battles, executions and hunting.

From about 640 BCE, civil wars between members of the royal family weakened Assyria. In 612 BCE they were defeated by an alliance of Babylonians and Medes, and were completely wiped out.

Leaders in war

Royal wealth was increased by success in making war, which brought in plunder and slaves. In addition to their religious roles, kings were usually expected to lead armies in battle. Warfare became a much more organised affair with the development of civilisations. Armies grew as states expanded and clashed with one another, or with the nomadic (wandering) peoples who were attracted by their wealth. A king's personal standing depended on being victorious and, in the ancient world, monarchs are often portrayed trampling on their enemies. After one famous battle at Kadesh in Syria (1274 BCE), both sides – Egyptians and Hittites – claimed to have triumphed. If, as seems likely, the result was actually a draw, the famous victory monuments put up by the pharaoh Ramesses II are an early example of propaganda designed to impress the people.

Despite their supposedly sacred character, monarchs could lose their thrones and dynasties could disappear. Such changes could happen very quickly. The first Chinese emperor, Shi Huangdi

> **If the ruler is upright [just], the people will imitate him as grass bends before the breeze.**

The Chinese philosopher Confucius (c.551–479 BCE) on the role of a monarch.

(*see page 11*), kept a firm grip on power until his death in 210 BCE. But then hatred of his harsh rule flared up. Soon his descendants had perished and a rebel leader founded a new dynasty, the Han (202 BCE–220 CE). But the idea of an emperor, 'the Son of Heaven', ruling over China, lasted for 2,000 years, right down to 1911.

Europe

The first European civilisations appeared around 2200 BCE on the island of Crete, and then, about 1600 BCE, in mainland Greece. Little is known of Cretan history, but the early Greeks, or Mycenaeans, were organised into formidable, warrior-dominated kingdoms.

However, the great age of Greece began much later (in the eighth century BCE) and was based on city-states – relatively small states, each with a single city at its heart. Some of them were monarchies at first, but these were soon replaced. The Greeks

The first European civilisation grew up around 2200 BCE on the island of Crete in the eastern Mediterranean. The picture shows a reconstruction of the throne room of the palace at Knossos, based on archaeological finds.

Hero kings

The earliest Greeks, the Mycenaeans, flourished between about 1600 and 1150 BCE. Little is known of their deeds, but they appear in the *Iliad*, the first great literary work in Greek – and European – history. The *Iliad* is an epic poem by Homer. It was first written down in the eighth century BCE, but was composed earlier. It describes episodes in the war between the Greeks and the Trojans. The war famously ended when Greek warriors hid inside a gigantic wooden horse that the Trojans were fooled into taking inside their besieged city. The Greek warriors came out at night, opened the gates to their comrades, and the Trojans were massacred. Greek royal leaders such as Agamemnon of Mycenae and Nestor of Pylos featured in many legends.

invented a number of new political systems, including one in which all the citizens (but this meant males only, and not slaves) took part in government. The Greeks called this arrangement 'democracy'. Athens became the most celebrated ancient democracy, leading Greek resistance to the greatest monarchy of its time, the Persian Empire.

By the fourth century BCE, the Greek city-states' days of glory were over. They were dominated by Macedon, a neighbouring state that had adopted Greek ways but remained a monarchy. Led by King Alexander of Macedon, who became known as Alexander the Great, the Macedonians and Greeks conquered the Persian Empire and most of the known world by 325 BCE. Alexander died in 323 BCE, when he was only 33. His empire rapidly broke up into a handful of large Middle-Eastern Greek kingdoms, almost constantly at war with one another. But his conquests spread the Greek language and Greek culture over a huge area.

> **" Monarchy is the one system of government where power is used for the good of all. "**
>
> *This statement was written by the Greek philosopher Aristotle in the fourth century BCE, and has often been quoted in praise of monarchy. However, Aristotle was referring to benevolent monarchs who ruled for the benefit of their subjects. Aristotle contrasted monarchy with tyranny, the kind of monarchy in which the king rules for his own benefit. Clearly Aristotle recognised that there had been both good and bad monarchs.*

The Roman Empire

Meanwhile Rome, a small city-state in Italy, was gradually becoming stronger. Rome began as a monarchy, but in about 510 BCE its king was driven out and a republic was set up. The event is known from legend rather than factual history, but hatred of the idea of a king became a Roman tradition.

Over the centuries, the Roman Republic conquered lands all round the Mediterranean Sea. But governing such a vast empire was too much for the republic. Power passed to military leaders, and after long and bloody civil wars, the most successful general, Julius Caesar, became ruler of the Roman world. Although Caesar refused the title 'king', a group of conspirators, who believed that one-man rule would destroy the republic, assassinated him.

After further civil wars, Caesar's great-nephew, Augustus, emerged victorious in 30 BCE. He claimed to have restored the Roman Republic, and he made sure the old republican traditions were honoured. But in reality Augustus had concentrated

Hail, Caesar!

Julius Caesar's great achievements led to his family name, Caesar, becoming one of the titles used by Roman emperors – even those who were not related to him. Even in the early twentieth century, the emperors of Germany and Russia were known as the Kaiser and the Tsar, both versions of 'Caesar'. The words 'emperor' and 'imperial' come from the Latin 'imperator', meaning 'commander', a title used by the Roman emperor Augustus and his successors. Augustus avoided the title 'king' because Romans hated the word. There has never been a clear-cut difference between a king and an emperor, but 'emperor' tends to be used by the rulers of very large states, especially if there are many different subject peoples in them.

power in his own hands and ruled as he pleased. The kingly title was never revived, but Augustus and his successors became known as emperors.

The Roman emperors had a very mixed record. The bloodthirsty, reckless careers of Caligula (37–41 CE) and Nero (54–68 CE) have led some historians to believe they were insane. By contrast, 'five good emperors' were said to have made the second century CE a Roman golden age of peace and prosperity. Later emperors were often successful generals who seized the throne, gaining or losing power while the empire was increasingly menaced by peoples outside it. In the fourth century, the empire became Christian, and one result was to strengthen the emperor's authority as a ruler chosen by God and blessed by the Church. This important development carried over into Europe even when Roman power collapsed and a new age began from the fifth century onwards.

These scenes of the all-conquering Roman army are among the many carved on to Trajan's Column in Rome, Italy, in 113 CE. The carvings are the Romans' own record of the campaigns in Dacia (modern Romania) conducted by the Emperor Trajan (98–117 CE). The methodical way in which the soldiers are constructing fortifications, and their discipline as they prepare to take ship, display some of the qualities that made Rome great.

CHAPTER 3
The Rise and Decline of Monarchy

In the fifth century, the western part of the Roman Empire broke up. Germanic tribes, often described as Barbarians, took control from Britain to North Africa, setting up their own kingdoms. The eastern part of the Roman Empire survived. Once separated from the Roman and Latin west, it became increasingly Greek in character, and it is generally known under the Greek name of Byzantium. But in the seventh century most of Byzantium's Middle Eastern and North African territories were conquered by Arab invaders, inspired by the religion of Islam preached by the prophet Muhammad. Soon, the Islamic Empire stretched from Persia to southern Spain. Byzantium remained a force to be reckoned with, its territories including Anatolia (modern Turkey) and south-east Europe.

Byzantium and the Islamic Empire (or Caliphate) were ruled by monarchs who wielded supreme political and religious authority. One of the Byzantine emperor's titles was 'Autocrator' (autocrat, our word, comes from the Greek original), while the caliph (Islamic ruler) was known as the 'Commander of the Faithful'.

This map shows the Byzantine Empire and the extent of Islamic Arab conquests by about 700 CE

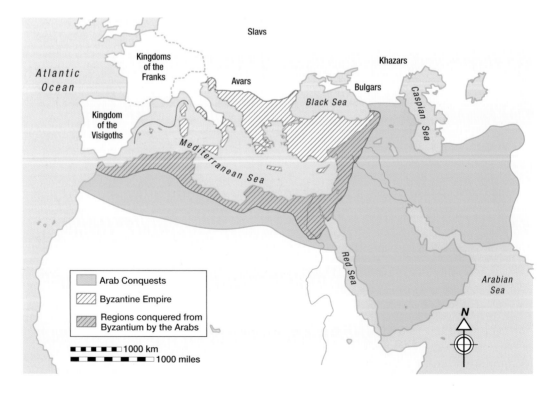

Slavs

Kingdoms of the Franks

Atlantic Ocean

Kingdom of the Visigoths

Avars

Khazars

Bulgars

Black Sea

Caspian Sea

Mediterranean Sea

Red Sea

Arabian Sea

N

Arab Conquests

Byzantine Empire

Regions conquered from Byzantium by the Arabs

1000 km
1000 miles

'Barbarian' Europe

The Germanic kings of Europe had nothing like this authority, and their war-torn realms were backward by comparison with the Byzantine and Islamic empires. The Germanic kings were at first little more than tribal war leaders, elected by their companions in arms. The kings were usually chosen from a single family, but there was no automatic succession by inheritance. In particular, a child had little chance of succeeding in the rough, post-Roman world, or, if he did, he rarely survived for long. In the Germanic kingdoms, the Church generally supported the monarchy, devising ceremonies that emphasised its sacred character. Even so, among Germanic peoples such as the Franks and the Visigoths, kingship was a dangerous occupation and their history is filled with treacheries, assassinations and massacres.

After centuries of wars, migrations and invasions by outside peoples, Europe began to settle down and distinct national groups such as the French and Germans evolved. Around 1000, Europe entered the period known as the Middle Ages, which lasted until about 1500. The hereditary nature of kingship became more firmly established, but royal powers were still limited by lack of resources, poor communications, and the political and social system. Medieval monarchs sometimes behaved badly, but law and custom generally restricted their actions. The nobility, the Church, towns and other bodies had 'liberties' (privileges) and rights that monarchs could not interfere with. In many states, monarchs found it wise to listen to the opinions of councils of leading men or assemblies of people representing various classes (for example, the English parliament and similar bodies in France and Scotland).

In time, nations such as England, France and Scotland became united under their own kings. But in Germany and Italy there were many states, widely

New peoples in Europe around 500 CE: an episode in the lives of Clovis, king of the Franks, and Alaric, king of the Visigoths.

ROME REVIVED

Charlemagne (768–814 CE), the king of the Franks, created the first great European empire since the fall of Rome. The areas that are now France, Germany, northern Italy and north-eastern Spain all fell under his rule. In 800, Charlemagne rescued the head of the Catholic Church, Pope Leo III, from his enemies. The grateful pope crowned Charlemagne emperor in Rome on Christmas Day, 800. This was intended to make Charlemagne and his heirs the sovereign of a renewed, Christian Roman Empire. In fact, after Charlemagne's death in 814 his empire was divided among his sons, but the idea of a revived empire was taken up again in the eleventh century, when it became known as the Holy Roman Empire.

different in size and influence. The Holy Roman Emperor (*see panel, left*) was the overlord of Germany and other parts of central Europe, but despite his grand title he had little control over individual states such as Saxony, Brandenburg and Bavaria, which became more, not less, independent over time. In Italy, the rival states included the central Italian territories ruled by the pope, the head of the Catholic Church.

'New Monarchies'

In the late Middle Ages, the monarchies of Western Europe gradually became more powerful. By the sixteenth century, this tendency was so marked that many historians describe states such as England, France and Spain as 'New Monarchies'.

Their 'newness' lay in their increasing resources and greater ability to control their subjects. Royal government became more efficient, conducted by well-trained bureaucracies – sets of officials who ran the state and collected taxes. 'Liberties' were removed, and royal law was imposed everywhere in the realm. The great nobles submitted to royal authority and served it, or were humbled. The Church, too, lost much of its non-spiritual power. A royal army made sure that royal policy was enforced. This army was generally stronger than any opposing local force of noble retainers or rebellious commoners.

The growth in royal authority took place over a long period and often experienced setbacks. But the strengthening of state power was based on many favourable developments, including economic expansion, the increasing cost of waging war, and the sixteenth-century Reformation, a religious movement which divided Christians into Catholics and Protestants and weakened the churches' ability to resist state control.

Trained civil servants extended the power of the 'New Monarchies' of sixteenth-century Europe. Here, an English tax collector is making sure that the state receives its due.

This picture shows Montezuma, emperor of the Aztecs in Central America. The arrival of the Spanish in 1520 led to his death and the destruction of Aztec civilisation.

American emperors
The Americas have been inhabited for at least 20,000 years, and advanced societies appeared there by 1150 BCE. When Europeans arrived in the early sixteenth century, there were two great American civilisations which had recently been united into empires – by the Aztecs in Central America, and the Incas in Peru and neighbouring territories in South America. Although they were far apart, the position of their monarchs was similar. The Aztec and Incan emperors were such sacred figures that their subjects were forbidden to look them in the face. Yet in the 1520s and 1530s small groups of Spanish adventurers were able to overthrow both empires. One reason for their success was that in each case they seized the emperor and ruled through him. The people only began to resist when it was too late. The Aztecs' and Incas' independence was lost and their religion and whole way of life were destroyed.

During the same period, Europeans developed ocean-going ships and began to explore the New World and trade directly with Africa and Asia. As a result, Europeans came into contact with monarchies of different types, including the Aztec emperors of Mexico and the Incas of Peru.

Absolutism

The strengthening of the state continued into the seventeenth century, and monarchs benefited in status as well as power. This was the age of absolutism (unrestrained royal rule), the most celebrated example being King Louis XIV of France, who was the dominant figure in Europe for most of his long reign (1643–1715).

Louis was served by able ministers, but he – not they – made the vital decisions. The king's personal power was so great that a letter sent by him was enough to have a man put in prison for an indefinite period. On the other hand, the European tradition of respect for law and custom was very strong, and in practice these put limits on royal power. Absolutism, despite its literal meaning, was not the same as autocracy.

Monarchs and republics

England was an exception to the absolutist trend. Kings and queens of the Tudor dynasty such as Henry VIII (1509–47) and Elizabeth I (1558–1603) strengthened the state, but worked with parliament. This meant that laws continued to be passed, and taxes to be raised, jointly by king and parliament. So when political and religious conflicts developed, parliament was strong enough to challenge the crown. The parliamentary forces won a civil war (1642–49), King Charles I was beheaded, and for a few years England was a republic. In 1660 King Charles II was restored to the throne, but in 1688 another political-religious crisis led to the exile of his brother, King James II. This, the 'Glorious Revolution' of 1688, was consolidated by new laws passed by parliament. These created a political system in which both crown and parliament had important roles, with policies formed by ministers who needed the support of both institutions. This type of monarchy, in which the crown has strictly defined legal powers, is known as a constitutional monarchy.

A scene from the English Civil War, 1645: the parliamentary leader, Oliver Cromwell, storms a royalist stronghold.

Names and numbers

The supporters of a monarchy believe in its right to rule. If it falls, they behave as though the new sovereign or government did not exist. As far as they are concerned, the fallen monarch continues to rule, followed by his, or her, descendants. This explains some curious numberings of monarchs.

Louis XVI (Sixteenth) was deposed during the French Revolution and executed in 1793. Eventually, in 1814, the monarchy was restored and his brother became king – as Louis XVIII (Eighteenth). As far as royalists were concerned, Louis XVI's small son had reigned as Louis XVII (Seventeenth), although he was held prisoner until he died, within a year or two of his father, at about the age of ten. Similarly, the Emperor Napoleon I was succeeded by his nephew, who called himself Napoleon III (1852–70), although Napoleon I's son had also never ruled.

In 1707, England and Scotland were united to create the kingdom of Great Britain. The term 'Britain' has continued in common use, although from 1801, when Ireland became part of the state, the correct name was the United Kingdom. As a result of later political changes, the full name became the present 'the United Kingdom of Great Britain and Northern Ireland', which is commonly abbreviated to 'the UK'. Britain grew steadily stronger through the eighteenth and nineteenth centuries, pioneering the Industrial Revolution and acquiring an enormous overseas empire. During the same period, the powers of the monarch were gradually transferred to the elected government. Under Queen Victoria (1837–1901) Britain's modern constitutional monarchy took shape.

In North America, thirteen of Britain's colonies rebelled, and in 1783 they became independent as the United States of America (USA). This new republic represented the first important challenge to monarchy in modern times. Soon afterwards, a revolution in France led to the founding of a republic there. The French Republic was short-lived, although its basically democratic ideals continued to have a strong influence. The republic was replaced by a new French monarchy, the Empire. In a brief but spectacular career, General Napoleon Bonaparte made himself Emperor of the French (1805–14, 1815) and put members of his family on several European thrones. But with the defeat of Napoleon in 1815 the old dynasties were restored.

Napoleon Bonaparte early in his career of conquest, leading his troops across the Alps into Italy in 1800.

All kings is mostly rapscallions [rascals].

A scornful republican view from The Adventures of Huckleberry Finn *(1884) by the American writer Mark Twain.*

23

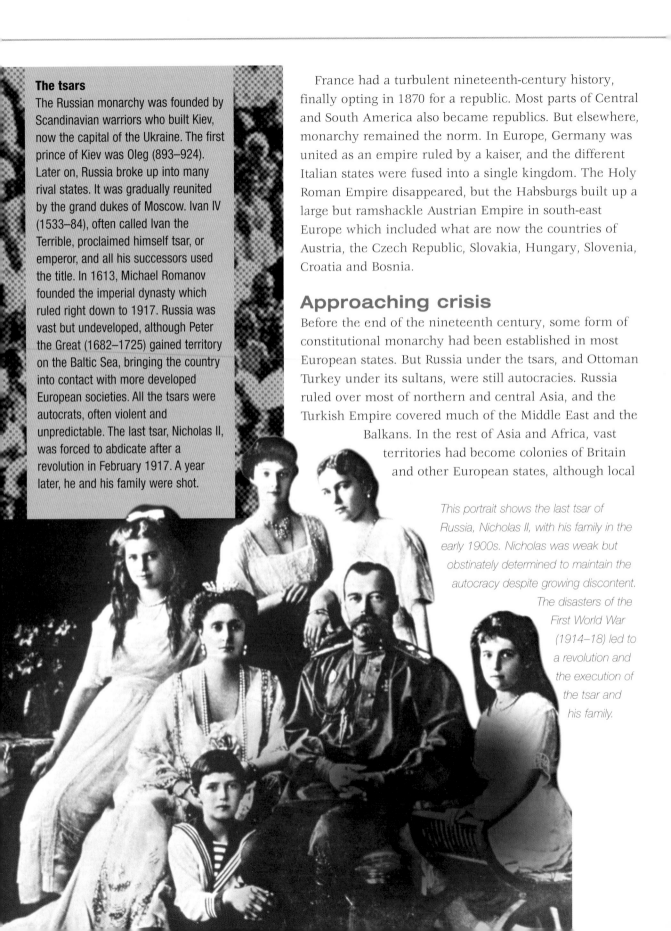

The tsars

The Russian monarchy was founded by Scandinavian warriors who built Kiev, now the capital of the Ukraine. The first prince of Kiev was Oleg (893–924). Later on, Russia broke up into many rival states. It was gradually reunited by the grand dukes of Moscow. Ivan IV (1533–84), often called Ivan the Terrible, proclaimed himself tsar, or emperor, and all his successors used the title. In 1613, Michael Romanov founded the imperial dynasty which ruled right down to 1917. Russia was vast but undeveloped, although Peter the Great (1682–1725) gained territory on the Baltic Sea, bringing the country into contact with more developed European societies. All the tsars were autocrats, often violent and unpredictable. The last tsar, Nicholas II, was forced to abdicate after a revolution in February 1917. A year later, he and his family were shot.

France had a turbulent nineteenth-century history, finally opting in 1870 for a republic. Most parts of Central and South America also became republics. But elsewhere, monarchy remained the norm. In Europe, Germany was united as an empire ruled by a kaiser, and the different Italian states were fused into a single kingdom. The Holy Roman Empire disappeared, but the Habsburgs built up a large but ramshackle Austrian Empire in south-east Europe which included what are now the countries of Austria, the Czech Republic, Slovakia, Hungary, Slovenia, Croatia and Bosnia.

Approaching crisis

Before the end of the nineteenth century, some form of constitutional monarchy had been established in most European states. But Russia under the tsars, and Ottoman Turkey under its sultans, were still autocracies. Russia ruled over most of northern and central Asia, and the Turkish Empire covered much of the Middle East and the Balkans. In the rest of Asia and Africa, vast territories had become colonies of Britain and other European states, although local

This portrait shows the last tsar of Russia, Nicholas II, with his family in the early 1900s. Nicholas was weak but obstinately determined to maintain the autocracy despite growing discontent. The disasters of the First World War (1914–18) led to a revolution and the execution of the tsar and his family.

kings and chiefs were sometimes left in place, under the 'protection' of the colonial power. Some states did manage to keep their independence, notably the Chinese and Japanese empires and the kingdom of Thailand.

Still apparently dominant in 1900, monarchy was almost destroyed by the upheavals of the twentieth century. In 1911, a revolution overthrew the 2,000-year-old Chinese Empire. The First World War of 1914–18 led to the collapse of the German, Austro-Hungarian, Russian and Turkish empires. After the Second World War (1939–45), the monarchs of Italy and Eastern Europe lost their thrones. In the 1940s and 1950s, changes in the Arab world replaced most of its monarchies with republics. And as the former colonies of the European empires became independent between 1945 and 1975, most of them chose to become republics. As late as 1973, a European monarchy, Greece, was abolished.

The remaining monarchies include some powerful and important states. And they continue to be remarkably varied, as is shown in the next chapter.

Monarchs in exile: Manuel II of Portugal (centre) and his mother with Alfonso XIII of Spain, leaving London's Ritz hotel in the 1930s.

1918
Germany: on 9 November, Kaiser Wilhelm II abdicates and flees as revolution breaks out and Germany slides to defeat in the First World War. The kings of Bavaria, Württemberg and Saxony also lose their thrones

Austria-Hungary: on 11 November, as his defeated empire falls apart, Charles I abdicates

1931
Spain: King Alfonso XIII is overthrown and a republic declared. (But his son, Juan Carlos I, is restored in 1975.)

1946
Italy: the monarchy is discredited by its role in the Second World War. In June King Umberto II leaves after Italians vote for a republic

Bulgaria: in September, King Simeon II is exiled after a communist takeover

1973
Greece: King Constantine (in exile since 1967) abdicates when Greeks vote against the return of the monarchy

1900   1925   1950   1975

1910
Portugal: King Manuel II flees following a national revolt

1917
Russia: Tsar Nicholas is forced to abdicate after the Russian Revolution; he and his family are shot in 1918

1939
Albania: King Zog I flees as the country is invaded by Italy

1945
Yugoslavia: King Peter II, in exile since 1941, is deposed as communists take power

1947
Romania: communists overthrow King Michael I

TIMELINE: THE FALL OF EUROPEAN MONARCHIES IN THE TWENTIETH CENTURY

CHAPTER 4

Modern Monarchies

Today there are relatively few monarchies, but they are still found all over the globe. In Europe there are seven kingdoms, all of them constitutional monarchies.

European monarchies

The UK consists of England, Wales, Scotland and Northern Ireland, countries brought together over the centuries by conquest or dynastic marriages. The present sovereign is Queen Elizabeth II (born 1926). The long history of the monarchy, and the way in which it has adapted to democratic institutions, are reflected in splendid ceremonies, and in political forms and traditions that have been left over from the past.

As a result, British monarchs still appear to be very powerful. The monarch can declare war and appoint ministers, and has many other government powers (known as the royal prerogative). The monarch is also part of the law-making process. Laws are made by 'the Queen in Parliament' and all need the queen's assent (agreement).

The reality of the situation is very different. A British monarch does not take any important political decision. She or he always acts on 'advice', usually the advice given by the current prime minister. So it is the prime minister or the government that actually takes the decisions and makes use of the prerogative and other royal powers. This is one reason why the term 'the crown' is so often used: it avoids any suggestion that the queen is personally involved, for example in a legal case brought by 'the crown' (the state prosecutors). Since the government takes all political decisions, the Queen cannot be blamed for them. She is regarded as being 'above politics'; she takes no sides, and can therefore be seen as commanding the loyalty of the entire people.

As a rule, all political responsibility falls on the elected government. But prime ministers can benefit from the advice of an experienced monarch,

Not British

Two places in the British Isles, the Isle of Man and the Channel Islands, are not part of the UK, although they owe allegiance to the crown. English monarchs once also held the separate title of dukes of Normandy, a region in France. But in 1205 the French king conquered all of mainland Normandy. The Channel Islands were all that was left of the duchy, and therefore they belong to the crown but are not part of Britain. The Isle of Man and the Channel Islands have their own assemblies (equivalent to Britain's parliament) and run their own affairs, but the British government takes charge of their defence and foreign relations.

and it is just possible that, in some unusual situation, the monarch might have to intervene. This occurred during a political and economic crisis in 1930, when King George V persuaded the prime minister, Ramsey Macdonald, to stay in office and try to form a new 'national' government. Macdonald did so, with important consequences, including a split in his own Labour Party which changed the entire balance of political forces.

The once-enormous British Empire disappeared in the late twentieth century, as peoples in Britain's colonies won their independence. Now only a handful of overseas territories, such as Gibraltar and the Falkland Islands, are

Britain's Queen Elizabeth II makes the Speech from the Throne in 2003; her husband, Prince Philip, is seated beside her.

Royal duties

Most of a constitutional monarch's actions are symbolic or ceremonial, which means they do not affect politics. Britain's Queen Elizabeth II opens parliament at the beginning of every annual session. She then reads the Speech from the Throne – a speech which is written for her by the government and outlines its future policies. She has to sign Acts of Parliament (the royal assent) before they become law. She confers knighthoods and other honours (acting on government advice). She also meets foreign ambassadors, makes goodwill visits as head of state to other countries, and keeps in touch with her subjects by being present on all sorts of occasions such as the opening of a new hospital or the staging of a popular sporting event. The Queen's political duties involve reading state documents and a weekly meeting with the prime minister.

WELCOMES
MAJESTY QUEEN ELIZABETH II

still under British rule. Many former British colonies belong to the Commonwealth, a friendly association of fully independent states. The British monarch is the head of the Commonwealth, but the position is purely honorary.

However, there are also fifteen ex-imperial countries that are now independent, but have chosen to retain the Queen as head of state – that is, holding the same position as she holds in Britain. She therefore reigns as a constitutional monarch in each of these sixteen countries (including the UK), which are quite separate from one another. Since she cannot be in more than one place at a time, she resides in Britain and is represented in each of the other countries by a governor-general, who carries out all the royal duties. The governor-general is appointed by the Queen on the advice of the government of the country in question. Queen Elizabeth is currently the sovereign of Canada, Australia and New Zealand; of many states in or close to the Caribbean, namely Belize and the island nations of Jamaica, Antigua and Barbuda, the Bahamas, Barbados, Grenada, St Kitts and Nevis, St Lucia, and St Vincent and the Grenadines; and of three other island states, Papua New Guinea, the Solomons and Tuvalu. All of these states have democratic parliamentary systems similar to Britain's, and the crown has a similar role in each of them.

Jamaican children greet Britain's Queen Elizabeth II with enthusiasm as she passes through the island's capital, Kingston, in 2002. The trip was part of the celebrations marking her fiftieth anniversary as queen.

❝ To advise, to encourage, and to warn. ❞

These were the political duties of the British monarch according to Walter Bagehot's influential book The English Constitution, *published in 1867.*

Continental kingdoms

Six European kingdoms are run on broadly similar lines to the UK, however different the ceremonial trappings may be (Norway, for example, has no coronation). In other words, royal prestige is great but the elected government exercises any powers that the monarch may have as head of state.

Denmark has been a monarchy since the tenth century. One of its kings, Cnut (Canute), also ruled England and Norway. Females have been allowed to inherit the throne since 1952, making it possible for the present monarch, Margrethe, to become queen in 1972. Norway was an independent kingdom during the early Middle Ages, but from the fourteenth century it was dominated by Denmark or Sweden. In 1905, Norway broke away from Sweden, electing a Danish prince as its king.

The Swedish kingdom is also ancient, though it was overshadowed by Denmark until the seventeenth century, when Sweden was briefly a major military power controlling wide territories around the Baltic Sea. Present-day Sweden is strongly democratic and committed to equality. The constitution firmly states that the monarch is head of state but takes no part in government. And the eldest child, whether male or female, inherits the throne (unlike most monarchies, where preference is given to the male).

Dots on the map

There are four tiny European monarchies that are easily overlooked on a map: the principalities of Andorra, Liechtenstein and Monaco, and the Grand Duchy of Luxembourg. All are constitutional monarchies, but because of their small size, the wealth and prestige of the ruling family tends to have considerable influence. In Liechtenstein, where the importance of the financial industry creates special circumstances, voters agreed in 2003 to increase the prince's powers after he threatened to move out of the country. The strangest arrangement is found in Andorra, which is ruled by 'co-princes'. These are now the president of France and the bishop of Urgel in northern Spain!

England, June 2002: a gathering of the reigning sovereigns of Europe and their husbands and wives. They are celebrating the Golden Jubilee of Queen Elizabeth II (centre), who came to the throne in 1952.

An independent Netherlands was created in 1598, when the provinces of what are now the Netherlands and Belgium revolted against Spanish rule. Only the seven northern provinces were successful, becoming the Dutch Republic or Netherlands. For centuries, the Orange family occupied the highest political and military office in the republic; its members included the William of Orange who became king of England (1689–1702) in partnership with his wife Mary. In 1815, a member of the Orange family became the first king of the Netherlands as William I (1815–40). The Netherlands is another monarchy where succession to the throne is in order of birth, irrespective of sex.

After the 1598 revolt, Spain reconquered the provinces to the south of the Netherlands. They were ruled in turn by Spain, Austria and the Netherlands until 1830, when they broke away from the Netherlands, took the name Belgium, and invited a German prince (Leopold, uncle of Britain's Queen Victoria) to become king.

Spain became a united and powerful kingdom in the late fifteenth century and spearheaded the European discovery and conquest of the Americas. But Spain's

In April 2004, King Juan Carlos speaks to the Spanish parliament in Madrid at its opening session. The atmosphere is markedly less formal than in the equivalent British scene on page 27.

ROYAL DEMOCRAT

Spain's turbulent history has caused King Juan Carlos I to play a much more active political role than most European monarchs. Spain became a republic in 1931, but after the ferocious Spanish Civil War (1936–39), the victor, General Francisco Franco, established a military dictatorship. Franco did not restore the monarchy during his lifetime, but he arranged that Juan Carlos should become king after his death, which took place in 1975. Franco believed that Juan Carlos would maintain the general's anti-democratic brand of conservatism. But Juan Carlos chose advisers who helped him to move cautiously towards a democratic Spain, established in the constitution of 1978. Later, in 1981, a lieutenant-colonel in the Civil Guard held the entire Spanish parliament as hostages, intending to start an anti-democratic revolution. The king's firm opposition to the plot was an important factor in its rapid collapse. Since then, Spain has functioned as a stable constitutional monarchy.

sixteenth-century 'Golden Age' was followed by a long decline. In the nineteenth century, the monarchy became involved in the civil wars fought between rival political groups. Further conflicts devastated twentieth-century Spain until a constitutional monarchy was established under King Juan Carlos I (1975–).

The Middle East

Most of the Middle East was ruled between the fourteenth and nineteenth centuries by the sultans of the Ottoman Turkish Empire. Separate kingdoms developed in the region as the Turkish Empire weakened, and others were set up after it fell in 1922. Many of these monarchies were replaced by republics in the late twentieth century, but some have so far survived the political upheavals of the region.

The largest Middle Eastern monarchy is Saudi Arabia, a mainly desert kingdom which extends over most of the Arabian peninsula. It was created by Ibn Saud, who conquered a number of previously separate territories between 1913 and 1925. In 1932 the royal family's name, Saud, became part of the kingdom's title. Since then, Saudi Arabia has become wealthy, thanks to its vast

Holy monarch
The Vatican City State is almost impossible to classify. It is the world's smallest state, effectively a palace in the middle of the Italian capital, Rome. The pope, the head of the worldwide Roman Catholic Church, lives in the Vatican. As the absolute sovereign of the city state and its approximately 900 inhabitants, he can be described as a monarch. But the papal monarchy is unusual, since popes are elected (by an assembly of cardinals) and there is no hereditary aspect to this essentially spiritual office.

The Saudi Crown Prince (heir to the throne), Abdullah bin Abdul Aziz, on a visit to Pakistan in October 2003. He inspects an honour guard of Pakistani soldiers in the capital, Islamabad.

Asia

As in the Middle East, monarchies in Asia have not found it easy to deal with conflicts between tradition and the demands of the modern world. The most successful has been Japan, for the surprising reason that it was defeated in the Second World War (1939–45) and then occupied. The emperor, previously worshipped as a divine being, was forced by the US and its allies to admit publicly that this was not so. The 1947 constitution recognised him as the symbol of the nation, but denied him any political role. Since then, Japan has functioned as a prosperous parliamentary democracy.

Four of Asia's seven monarchies are situated in South-east Asia. In Thailand the monarchy has existed since 1782, and was absolute until 1932. It has remained widely revered by ordinary Thais, but has played an unclear role in politics. Parliamentary systems have been established and scrapped many times, not by the king but by the army. In the early 2000s there were hopeful signs that Thailand was beginning to develop into a working constitutional monarchy, although, as yet, political parties were not allowed.

The royal line continues: in 2002, King Bhumibol and Queen Sirikit of Thailand take part in the ceremony in which their grandchild is named.

Neighbouring Cambodia has an extraordinary history. It became independent of France in 1953, but its king, Norodom Sihanouk, disliked his lack of power as a constitutional monarch. He abdicated and began a career as a politician. In the 1970s and 1980s a long period of bloodshed and chaos followed, at its worst in 1975–8, when the communist Khmer Rouge were responsible for mass killings. Subsequently the Cambodians were so bitterly divided that the United Nations took over the country and set up a new, democratic political system. It began to function in 1993 with a now aged Norodom Sihanouk reoccupying the throne – a royal recovery that is unprecedented in modern times.

Malaysia, to the south of Thailand, is a federation. A federation consists of a number of states or provinces which have united while continuing to control many of their own affairs (the USA, Canada and Australia are among the world's other federations). The Malaysian states have an unusual system for electing their supreme head. The rulers of the seven mainland states elect one of their number to the position, and he serves a five-year term. He is a constitutional monarch, since most decisions are taken by the elected Malaysian government.

The remaining three Asian monarchies are very small. In Brunei, on the island of Borneo, the sultan wields absolute power. As in the Gulf States, this is more easily tolerated because the possession of oil reserves has given Brunei a very high standard of living. In two relatively remote Himalayan kingdoms, Nepal and Bhutan, royal and religious traditions remain strong, though from the 1990s moves were made in both countries to give the people a greater say.

In the Pacific area, the island group of Samoa is a constitutional monarchy. Its king is head of state for life, but future heads of state will be elected for five-year terms. In Tonga, the tradition-based authority of the king is very great. In the assembly, elected members are a minority and unitl 2005, all cabinet members were handpicked by the king outside parliament.

Asian dynasties

- China had a long history of kingdoms and dynasties even before Shi Huangdi united the country in 221 BCE. Famous imperial dynasties included the Han (202 BCE–220 CE), the Tang (618–907), the Song (960–1279), the Ming (1368–1644) and the Qing or Manchus (1644–1912). China became a republic in 1911.

- Japan's first emperor was the legendary Jimmu (c.40 BCE). All subsequent Japanese emperors claimed to be descended from him. The present emperor is Akihito (1989–).

- The sub-continent of India has been ruled by many dynasties, though few have controlled the entire region. The Mughals invaded from central Asia, and Babur became emperor in 1526. After two centuries of splendour, Mughal power declined during the eighteenth century, while Britain grew progressively more powerful in the region. The last emperor, Bahadur Shah II, was dethroned by the British in 1858 for his part in the1857 rebellion (the 'Indian Mutiny').

- Korea's Yi dynasty ruled from 1392 until Japan annexed (took over) the country in 1910.

- The Konbaung dynasty of Burma (now Myanmar) reigned from 1752. The British dethroned the last king, Thibaw, in 1885.

- The present Thai dynasty dates from 1782.

- Laos was an ancient kingdom. Its last dynasty reigned from 1904 until the communist takeover in 1975.

- Vietnam's ruling dynasty (from 1802) ended in 1945, when Emperor Bao Dai abdicated.

CHAPTER 5

The Future of Monarchy

In the past, monarchies appeared wherever settled communities and town life developed. Myths and folktales described the exploits of hero-kings and evil tyrants. The fortunes of nations and peoples were often directly tied to dynasties as they rose and fell. Clearly, monarchy was an institution of central importance. But from the nineteenth century onwards, societies were transformed with amazing speed. By the early twenty-first century, some people were questioning whether monarchy had any further role to play.

There are now only a handful of absolute or politically powerful monarchies. These exist in countries where custom and tradition remain strong and change has been slow. But the outside world has already made an impact through technologies like television, computers, the Internet and mobile phones. This impact seems likely to grow stronger as large numbers of people become educated and prosperous, and expect to have a voice in the way their country is run. In the twenty-first century, the remaining absolute monarchies seem likely to yield to the now almost

Queen Elizabeth II is greeted by a host of Union flags on a visit to Aylesbury, Buckinghamshire, UK, in May 2002. Whatever the standing of other 'royals', she remains popular and respected.

universal belief that governments should be chosen by the people and answerable to them – in other words, the democratic spirit.

Constitutional monarchies appear to have much better prospects. They have worked well in countries where peaceful changes of government take place according to recognised rules. In these circumstances, the monarch can play a non-political role without difficulty. Monarchies are more vulnerable when there are upheavals, as happened in Greece in 1967, costing Constantine II his throne.

However, even in some politically stable constitutional monarchies, republicanism made some headway in the 1990s. Problems within Britain's royal family (*see page 41*) raised doubts about their role, and one respected newspaper, the *Guardian*, declared itself in favour of a republic. During the same period, a strong republican movement developed in Australia but failed in its bid to abolish the monarchy.

The republican argument

Most republicans do not oppose monarchy simply because of the way that individual monarchs behave. They believe that monarchy, including constitutional monarchy, is wrong in principle, based as it is on the idea that 'royal blood' is something special. Clearly monarchs are only special beings in so far as they have been shaped by lives of privilege and wealth. Almost everybody now agrees that a person's position in the world should be based on factors such as work, talent and achievement. Yet monarchs and royal families owe their position entirely to accidents of birth.

The existence of the monarchy also helps to maintain an undesirable division of society into ranks (dukes, earls, barons and other titles), similarly based on birth. Even

❝ Those who imagine that a politician would make a better figurehead than a hereditary monarch might perhaps make the acquaintance of more politicians. ❞

Baroness Margaret Thatcher, herself a politician (British prime minister 1979–90), in a speech made in 1985.

Republicanism in Australia
Queen Elizabeth II of Great Britain is also Queen of Australia. She is represented by a governor-general (and by governors of the individual states that make up Australia). Although Australians choose these officers, discontent with the monarchy has grown. In 1991, the Labor Party, then in power, came out in favour of a republic, and opinion polls consistently showed a majority of Australians agreeing. Republicans argued that a non-resident head of state could not adequately represent the country. They said that Australia was no longer mainly 'British' in outlook, and that monarchy conflicted with Australian beliefs in social and sexual equality. Campaigning on the issue was confused, with republicans divided about exactly what kind of head of state they wanted. Possibly for this reason, 55 per cent of voters favoured keeping the monarchy. The vote against was very large, and opinion polls continued to be pro-republican. Although current prime minister, Kevin Rudd, is a republican, he has indicated that no referendum will take place in the near future.

the language of monarchy is degrading to a free people, who are called subjects, not, as in a republic, citizens. The monarch is generally linked with a state religion, despite the fact that societies are increasingly filled with non-believers or people of many faiths. In this and in other ways, it has been argued, monarchies encourage a misguided and out-of-date view of society and the world.

The monarchist argument

Defenders of constitutional monarchies deny most of this. They claim that such arguments are based on abstract ideas rather than realities. They emphasise the importance of tradition in holding societies together. And they believe that when ordinary people express feelings of intense emotional loyalty towards royalty, this response is perfectly natural and valuable.

Monarchists may also argue that, in the real world, emotions are still focused on human leaders. In fact, support for dynasties is such a natural development that it often appears, unofficially, in republics. Three generations of the Nehru-Gandhi family governed India, with hardly a

UNLUCKY DYNASTY

India is one of several republics in which a single family has behaved very like a royal dynasty. Jawaharlal Nehru was a leading figure in the Indian struggle for independence from Britain. When independence was achieved in 1947, Nehru served as prime minister of India until his death in 1964. After only two years, Nehru's daughter, Mrs Indira Gandhi, began a long reign as prime minister (1966–77, 1980–84). Her son Sanjay was expected to succeed her, but after his death in an air crash, another son, Rajiv, was brought into politics. When Mrs Gandhi was assassinated in 1984, Rajiv became prime minister (1984–89). In 1991, while out of power, he too was assassinated. The magic of the 'dynasty' was so strong that in 1998 Rajiv's Italian-born wife Sonia was persuaded to lead the Gandhis' political party, Congress. It won the 2004 general election, although Sonia Gandhi refused to become prime minister.

India's ruling political 'dynasty' in 1950: Prime Minister Jawaharlal Nehru with his daughter Indira Gandhi and her son Rajiv, both future prime ministers.

US President John F. Kennedy poses for the press with his wife Jackie and their children at Easter 1963. The Kennedys were often described as the USA's 'royal family'.

break, from 1947. The Kennedy and Bush families have been remarkably prominent in US political life. And more than one woman has become president or prime minister of a country by being chosen to follow her husband in office, as if he were a hereditary monarch.

All of this suggests that the stability and continuity offered by a monarchy remains of importance in a democratic society. Governments may go through crises or become paralysed, but the monarchical head of state is always on duty. The hereditary succession ensures that there is no break between sovereigns and no dispute as to who should take on the office. Constitutional monarchs have no links with any political party, so people with all sorts of views can feel loyalty towards them. Key groups such as the armed forces, the police and the civil service benefit from feeling that, though they obey each government as it takes office, their final loyalty is to the crown, and through the crown to the people. In this way the monarch symbolises the nation, embodying its past glories and present unity.

❝The State functions more easily if it can be personified. An elected President who has stepped out of politics . . . is no substitute for a King who has stepped in by right of inheritance. Still less is an active politician, like the President of the United States, a substitute. We can damn the Government and cheer the King.❞

W. Ivor Jennings in his book, The British Constitution, *first published in 1943.*

King Christian X of Denmark is seen here in 1920, entering southern Jutland in triumph after the area voted to become part of Denmark. Later, the king and his white horse became symbols of Danish resistance to Nazi rule.

This unifying role may be particularly important in states where there are several groups with separate national traditions, for example in Britain (English, Welsh, Scottish and Irish) and in Belgium (Walloons and Flemings). And it is arguably more natural to feel an intense attachment to human beings than to an abstraction such as 'the republic'. Admirers of monarchy often refer to the nation-rallying role of the British royal family in the Second World War, when the country was being ravaged by German bombing. During the same conflict, King Christian X of Denmark set an example to his people after the conquest of his country by Nazi Germany. He encouraged non-co-operation with the occupiers, who eventually imprisoned him.

Monarchists also point out what they claim to be the weaknesses of a republican alternative. In a republic, the head of state is usually a president, who may be a powerful figure, as in the USA, or a figurehead, resembling an elected version of a constitutional monarch, as in Germany. In either case, he or she will stand for a political party or viewpoint opposed by many people, and will not represent the entire country. Where people distrust politicians, such a head of state will not arouse much enthusiasm.

Republicans, of course, disagree with most of these arguments. For example, they point out that, in the USA and France, republican institutions have not prevented their peoples from being passionately patriotic. The debate goes on. However, the fate of constitutional monarchies will probably not be decided by discussion, but by the popularity of royal individuals and families.

ROYAL COMEBACK

In 1989–90, the communist regimes of Eastern Europe collapsed. Democracies were set up in their place, and it was sometimes suggested that monarchies might be re-established in countries such as Russia and Romania. But so far the only real comeback has been in Bulgaria. In 1946 the communists abolished the monarchy and nine-year-old King Simeon II went into exile. Following the communist collapse, Simeon, now a successful businessman, was able to revisit Bulgaria. In 2001 he settled there permanently and organised a political party, the National Movement. In June 2001 it won a general election, and the ex-king became prime minister of Bulgaria, no longer Simeon II but using his family name, Simeon Borisov Sakskoburggotski.

Models or celebrities?

Constitutional monarchies have certainly adapted themselves to the great social changes of the past century. In 1900, monarchs were splendid, bemedalled and bejewelled figures, remote from the mass of the people. In the course of the twentieth century, this side of monarchy was maintained on great state occasions, but royal families increasingly took on a more 'ordinary' image. They frequently appeared in everyday clothing and had more contact with their subjects through activities such as visiting factories and attending sporting events. The monarchies of the Netherlands and Scandinavia cultivated this

Princess Diana (pictured here in 1997) was wife of Charles, Prince of Wales. At once glamorous and apparently 'ordinary', she was much admired. The British royal family's popularity suffered when they were rumoured to have treated her badly.

Unequal partners

Only one person normally inherits a throne. The husband or wife of that person is known as his, or her, consort. Confusingly, both a female monarch who reigns in her own right and the wife of a king may be called a queen. But the husband of a reigning queen is not called a king. Perhaps the best-known male royal consort was Queen Victoria's husband, 'the Prince Consort', Prince Albert (lived 1819–61), who played a prominent part in British life. More recent examples include Prince Bernhard (1911–2004), husband of Queen Juliana of the Netherlands, and Philip, Duke of Edinburgh (born 1921), who is married to Britain's Queen Elizabeth II.

PRINCESS DIANA

Diana, Princess of Wales, was the most famous and popular royal figure of recent times. In 1981, as Lady Diana Spencer, she married the heir to the British throne, Charles, Prince of Wales. Carried to her wedding in a glass coach, she was seen as a 'fairy-tale princess' and subsequently lent glamour to many royal occasions. After her marriage to Charles failed, the couple separated in 1992 and were divorced in 1996. Diana remained a prominent figure, campaigning for good causes such as funding for the treatment of the disease AIDS. She was popular because of her 'touchy-feely' style, expressing emotion and making physical contact, which contrasted with the normal, stiffly dignified royal manner. Well-publicised personal difficulties and love affairs did not dent her popularity. In 1997, 36-year-old Diana and her companion, Dodi Fayed, were killed when their car crashed in Paris. There was an extraordinary, worldwide outpouring of grief and sympathy and, in Britain, criticism of the royal family's initially cool response. Whether the monarchy would suffer any long-term damage was hard to predict.

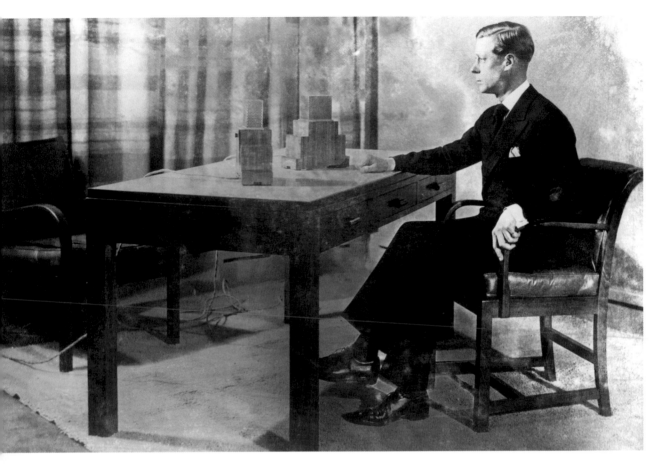

Edward VIII in March 1936, making his first radio broadcast as king. In December he would broadcast again, telling the British nation of his abdication.

'ordinary' image most thoroughly, but the British and other European monarchies were also affected by the trend.

However, the ordinariness of royal families was of a special, unblemished kind. They were – or were presented as – model families, happy and united. They were held up as an example to their peoples. In Britain this was true of the family lives of George V (1910–36), George VI (1936–52) and Elizabeth II (1952–). The standards they upheld were actually higher than those of ordinary people. By 1936, divorce was becoming acceptable, but when King Edward VIII insisted on marrying an American divorcée named Wallis Simpson he was forced to abdicate after reigning for less than a year. Even in 1955, Queen Elizabeth's sister, Princess Margaret, experienced similar pressures and gave up the idea of marrying a divorced man.

In the next few decades, standards changed very rapidly. Younger members of royal families were influenced by new social trends and more often made

Belgian breaks
Normally, the moment a monarch dies, the reign of the next monarch begins. However, present-day Belgium is an exception. There, the would-be king or queen must take an oath to the constitution before he or she can take office. This means that there are brief gaps between the reigns of Belgian monarchs.

personal choices (especially of marriage partners) that conflicted with traditional behaviour.

At the same time, the lives of royal individuals were investigated and described at length by newspapers, television and other media. In the past, the media had presented royalty in the most favourable light, often suppressing any unwelcome facts. But late twentieth-century journalists, equipped with tape recorders and zoom-lens cameras, fed the public with accounts of royal lapses, love affairs, quarrels and divorces.

The immediate effect was largely to destroy the perfect-family image of royalty. People who had idealised royal families were disillusioned. But all that had happened was that royalty were seen to have the same problems as other people; and this did not necessarily make them unpopular. In fact, royalty seemed to be becoming part of present-day 'celebrity culture', like the film stars whose escapades are followed by millions of people. So it is possible that royalty will settle into a new public role. Alternatively, more effective measures may be taken to safeguard the privacy of 'royals' and to influence the way they are perceived by the public.

It is clearly too soon to know how such developments will affect monarchy. Over the centuries, it has proved flexible enough to take on widely different roles, so it may well continue to find a place in the rapidly changing modern world.

A modern image of monarchy: Prince William, grandson of Queen Elizabeth II, is shown in 2003, casually dressed and kicking a ball on a beach in Scotland.

TIMELINE: MONARCHIES IN THE NEWS

1997
Diana, Princess of Wales, is killed in a car crash

2001
Norway's Crown Prince marries a single mother and former waitress; popular interest is great

During an argument, the Crown Prince of Nepal shoots the king and several other members of his family, then kills himself

Ex-king Simeon II becomes prime minister of his former kingdom, Bulgaria

2003
Electors in Liechtenstein vote to give the prince greatly extended powers

Protests force King Mswati III of poverty-stricken Swaziland to give up plans to buy an executive jet

2002
The emirate of Bahrain becomes a kingdom, with a new, more democratic constitution

The former Italian royal family, banished since 1946, are allowed to return. Prince Emmanuele Filiberto's marriage takes place in Rome in 2003 and is a great social and media event

2004
Prince Felipe of Spain marries Letizia Ortiz, a divorced former journalist

1997　1998　1999　2000　2001　2002　2003　2004

Index